I CAN POTTY
1 2 3

By Adriana Vermillion

For more information about potty training, the author, or bookings,

please visit

www.pottytrainingservices.com

or

www.adrianavermillion.com

Written by Adriana Vermillion
Illustrated by Bianca Paz
Published by P.O.T."Y" Generation®
ISBN: 978-1-940710-01-3

I would like to dedicate this book to my children, Nate and Abby
who inspire me to help others every day.

"Oh no! Mommy, I had
an accident!

"How can we have my Big Boy party if I couldn't stay dry?" Alex asked in tears.

"Once upon a time, there was
a little baby named Alex.

"That's okay, Alex," his mommy said, "We all have accidents sometimes, but it helps us learn. Let's clean up and I will tell you a story before our party begins."

"Baby Alex wore diapers,

ate from a bottle,

and crawled on the floor.

"When Alex grew older, he ate mushy foods,

started talking,

and walking.

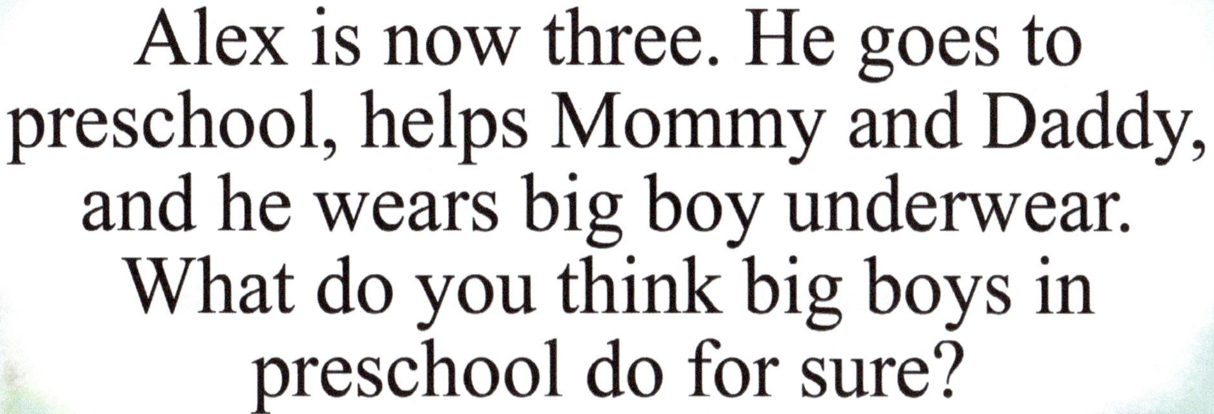

Alex is now three. He goes to preschool, helps Mommy and Daddy, and he wears big boy underwear. What do you think big boys in preschool do for sure?

"Hmm… be nice?"

"Yes! What else?"

"Be helpful?"

"Absolutely! Anything else?"

"How about stay dry?"

"You got it! Give me five."

"Ready for the party? Your friends will be here soon for your Big Boy day.

Can you please help me?"

"Yes, Mommy!"

Someone was knocking on the door.

"Mommy, Mommy, I think someone is at the door!"

"OK, let's go and
see."

Alex's friends came over
and the evening was off to
a great start.

Alex celebrated with his family and friends Daniel, Julia and Jonathan and took many potty breaks.

They wore party hats,

danced,

and shared some yummy cupcakes and juice.

Alex was now an official big boy
and excited to stay dry by
practicing on the big kid potty.

Alex said good-bye to
his friends

and went upstairs
with Mommy
and Daddy to get
ready for bed.

Mommy and Daddy had a big
surprise for him:

his very own underwear!

Because Alex was a big boy now,
he put all his baby toys, diapers,
and wipes in small boxes for other
babies who could use them.

Alex went potty,

washed his hands,

and brushed his teeth.

He was very happy to wear his big boy underwear to bed.

After a short bed-time story,

Alex gave Mommy and Daddy a big kiss,

and soon after he was fast asleep.

THE END!

www.ingramcontent.com/pod-product-compliance
Lightning Source LLC
Chambersburg PA
CBHW042136030726
47599CB00002B/489